Walking with Angels

Walking with Angels

The Answers Are There —

Janie Emerson

Cover Illustration by Laura Boardman

Copyright © 2002, 2025 Janie Emerson.
All rights reserved. This book or any portion thereof may not be reproduced or used in any manner whatsoever without the express written permission of the publisher except for the use of brief quotations in a book review.

ISBN: 978-0-9716320-2-8
Cover illustration by Laura Boardman
Book design by Janie Emerson
Printed in the United States of America.

JEM Enterprises
La Jolla, California

ShamrockWisdom.com

DEDICATED TO

My dear friend, Nanette,
whose passion and clarity
show me my "real me"
always –

INTRODUCTION

Everyone has angels in their lives.
They are our guides, our companions,
our confidants, and our protectors.

They are our "Life Angels."

They show us how to live. How to enjoy
every moment, to love with abandon,
and to be present always.
They "talk to us" all the time.

Share this book with your whole family.
Open to a page to learn from your special angels. They have so much to teach us
about living. Take time to be present,
to listen, and to learn from these
"Angel Words."

Walk with your angels every day…

Our Angels
walk
beside us
always ....

The
answers are
there.
When you are
ready,
reach for
them —

You
are surrounded
by
gentle, knowing —
You have
great
days ahead . . . .

Create miracles
from
your heart —
It is
what you
do
best —

Be happy
&
have fun —
That
is
the best of
life —

Relax
and let the
positive
energy flow
in
you now —

See
the miracles,
embrace them
and
believe them
all —

Have
laughs & joy
every day
no
matter what —

Focus
on
your goals
&
your dreams —
They
protect your
soul
always —

Freedom
is something you
feel within,
no
matter where
you are
or
what you are
doing —

Joy
is your
eternal medicine —
It
is your
soul energy —
It
is the real
you . . . .

Magic
is
when you can
truly
see each other
thru
open hearts —

Trust —
always trust
life's
abundance
and
plenty....

Wisdom
is
enjoying life's
simple
abundance
each day —

Keep
visualizing —
It
will become
part of you.
The
rest is easy . . . .

You
are reminded
that,
in all
circumstances,
it is
always
free choice —

You are
free
to choose every
moment
in
life to be
as
you want
it
to be . . . .

Attract
love,
peace,
joy,
health,
wealth
&
life!!!!

Your knowing
is
part of you —
It
needs no proof
It
quite simply
Is . . . .

It is
important to
honor
your dreams,
and
your beliefs . . . .

Yes,
you can make
life
perfect,
peaceful
&
prosperous
always —

It is not
for
you to change
others —
It is for
you
to be you
&
change will
come —

Face your
fears
and go
through them
to
wholeness . . . .

life is
your
choice —
So
soar with freedom
of
spirit
always —

You
are unlimited —
You
create miracles —
They are
yours to have
always —

Believing
is
essential —
It
creates success —

Nothing
is wasted —
It is
all part of
you . . . .

Recapture
the
living of
life
&
you will
be
whole —

To BE,
you
need beauty,
grace
&
balance.
They
are life's
oxygen —

Your
belief in miracles —
that
true grace
&
peaceful knowing —
is the
love
you have
within . . . .

Stay
to
your truth
with
love and joy.
It will
move mountains

Release
your identity
as
physically fragile —
it is
not you . . . .

Ask
nothing more than
to love
and be loved.
Then
totally enjoy
each
moment —

Real love
is
sharing your
true selves,
your souls,
&
your lives —

When you
relax & reach,
you
reconnect
as
one . . . .

The
magic moments
are
the light
that
sees you through
the
dark times . . . .

What
is most
important in life
is
to enjoy
every moment . . . .

Knowing
and feeling —
truly
feeling within —
are
totally different
realities . . . .

Joy
begets joy —
Health
begets health —
Happiness
begets happiness —

You are
protected and
made
strong
to
live life's
total joy —

You
know what
to do.
Laugh
&
enjoy
it all !!

life
is a constant
cleaning out —
Gently
releasing & embracing
to
form you . . . .

See
the "victim"
in
your life
&
release it,
gently,
with love —

Take
the time to
enjoy
the present —

With
clear intention
and
happy hearts
you will
move
forward —

To
thaw a broken,
closed heart
is
never easy
It
takes time and
love to
feel safe
again . . . .

The
answers are
there —
you will
see
them soon . . . .

Stay
to
your truth
and
be
vigilant —

Do what
you
need for
peace.
It
is the
key to
all life —

Release
worry & believe.
All
is now
well . . . .

Remember,
life
is energy —
You
can make it
anything
you want . . . .

Forge
the keys of
a
special life
with
your true
self —

It
is ok
to
remember,
but
release the
pain . . . .

All
you need
to do
is
just be
and
the joy of life
is there . . . .

You create
now
to love,
to heal,
and
to enjoy life
completely —

Be clear
&
your dreams
will
become
real —

Always
focus on what
is
most important —
It
is
your love . . . .

"Angel attitude"
is the
giggles of light
that
sparkle with
joyous
possibilities —

Let
your knowing
be
for you,
and
others' opinions
be
for them —

Life is
not about
control,
it is
about choices . . . .
Life is
not about
limits,
it is
about freedom . . . .

Taking
the freedom
to
live your life
is
important
for you . . . .

Your foundation
is the past —
Your vision
is the future —
Your life
is the now . . . .

The key
to life
is
to truly
"be yourself" —
All
else flows
from
that . . . .

If
you love life
it will
give you joy
&
great results —

To
touch hearts
is
special.
To
touch souls
is a
precious gift . . . .

Share
the
words & magic
with all —
It
will heal
many souls . . . .

Manifest
what
you want —
visualize it,
verbalize it,
&
believe it
as so . . . .

Time
to make your
choices
for
your reasons —

You
are brave —
you believed
&
you survived
by
holding to
your life . . . .

Trust
your heart
&
all else is
clear —

In
returning to
rest
you shall
be
saved —

Time
to shift the
energy
to
the positive —

Build
your life
on
real love
and
support —
Not jealousy
and control —

Freedom
&
responsibility
can
co-habitate —
It
depends where
one
puts the
emphasis —

Clarity
and
peace replace
the
past, and
envelope
the future . . . .

The
most important
question
is all
circumstances
is
"Why?"

Now
is the time
to be
about
wellness & health —
To be
free of
illness & fear —

Spread
your wings
&
take
your space!

Two
kindred spirits
fill the
void . . . .

Look
and see
the
miracle in
everything —
then
embrace it
totally . . . .

If you
want
your life,
your health,
your happiness
on
your terms —
Start
it now !

Sometimes
it
takes the
dark
to
give us
the
light —

Believe
in
your love
&
your power
no
matter what
they throw
at
you —

You are
a
powerful being
who
must be free
to
create
rather than
controlled
to be —

You
create
truth.
Remember
that
always . . . .

Miracles
are
the truth
of
Being —

Your vision
and
imagination
are
your special
gifts —
Trust them....

Be
appreciated,
accepted,
respected
on
your terms
always —

Just
clearly intend
and
the light will
shine
through —

Leave
struggle
to
others....

It is
by honoring
your process
&
your timing,
that
you move
forward....

To
have freedom —
take
responsibility
for
all you are . . . .

See
the good,
the fun,
&
the positive
in
all things
always —

No matter
what happens —
trust
what you feel
in each
moment —

It
is when
you
believe truly,
that
miracles come
to
you —

The quiet,
the beauty,
&
the power
to do
anything
is
your core . . . .

Step back —
Look
at all things
for
your reasons —
Then
proceed . . . .

The
goal is
to
have joy
with
life —

Always
be yourself,
no
matter what
the
situation . . . .

Never
give up
on
Your dreams —

It is
your right to
have —
freedom
joy
faith
trust
magic
& love . . . .

Use
the time given
wisely.
Remember it
is
your time
to
live —

ABOUT THE AUTHOR

JANIE EMERSON

Janie Emerson is the author of the successful *Appreciate Each Day*, *The Magic of Me*, and *My Special Girls*. Janie has written for newspapers, magazines, and won national awards for her poetry.

The inspiration for Janie's writings comes from life. It comes from her beloved Westies – from their joy and wisdom. Janie's work opens you to love and life. The intent is to empower, enhance, and make your life complete.

Janie was born and raised outside Philadelphia, on the Main Line, and in La Jolla, California. She is married to Bob, and lives with their special West Highland White Terriers (Westies).

Janie is a respected consultant and acclaimed speaker. She has been an advocate for women owned businesses nationally, an active community leader, and a successful breeder of top Champion Westies.

Janie is currently working on two new exciting projects.

www.ingramcontent.com/pod-product-compliance
Lightning Source LLC
Chambersburg PA
CBHW062057290426
44110CB00022B/2626